ESSENTIAL

P9-EDI-138

MANAGING MONEY
IN RETIREMENT

DALLAS SALISBURY
AND
MARC ROBINSON

DORLING KINDERSLEY
London • New York • Sydney • Delhi • Paris • Munich • Johannesburg

A DORLING KINDERSLEY BOOK

Editor Stephanie Rubenstein
Writing Les Abromovitz
Design and Layout Jill Dupont
Photography Anthony Nex
Project Editor Crystal A. Coble
Senior Art Editor Mandy Earey
Photo Research Mark Dennis, Sam Ruston
Indexing Rachel Rice
Editorial Director LaVonne Carlson
Design Director Tina Vaughan
Publisher Sean Moore

First American Edition, 2000
24681097531
Published in the United States by
Dorling Kindersley Publishing, Inc.
95 Madison Avenue,
New York, New York 10016

Packaged by Top Down Productions
Copyright © 2000
Dorling Kindersley Publishing, Inc.
Text copyright © 2000 Marc Robinson

**See our complete catalog at
www.dk.com**

A CIP catalog record for this book is available from the
Library of Congress

ISBN 0-7894-7174-4

Reproduced by Colourscan, Singapore
Printed by Wing King Tong, Hong Kong

CONTENTS

GENERATING INCOME

GROWING WHAT YOU HAVE

MANAGING YOUR MONEY

WHO CAN HELP?

INTRODUCTION

T he time you've dreamed about is finally here. You've retired. It's time to enjoy the fruits of your labor and pursue all of those dreams that were always put on the back burner while you were busy earning a living. Kick back and relax; you've earned it. If you want to be on the go every day, enjoy those activities as well. Just make sure you save a little time to manage your money in retirement. Managing Money in Retirement will tell you the most important things you need to know about saving for this most precious segment of your life. It will tell you what you need to consider, how various retirement plans work, who you can turn to for help, and some ways to be sure that you will be as comfortable as possible when you retire.

GETTING STARTED

Retirement can be a time of personal growth and new experiences—or you can fall into the same routine day after day. The choice is yours. While you may not have enough money to do everything you want, you can make the most of what you have.

WHAT WILL IT TAKE TO RETIRE?

Retirees typically live on 70 to 80 percent of their pre-retirement income. As you contemplate your vision of retirement and try to manage your money accordingly, keep these factors in mind.

YOUR MONEY MUST LAST

At the very least, your goal is to be able to spend what you need and make your money last the rest of your life. There are three basic ways you can make your money last:

- Protect what you have;
- Generate income;
- Grow your assets.

PEOPLE ARE LIVING LONGER

The Retirement Confidence Survey, which is conducted by the Employee Benefit Research Institute (EBRI), found that 18% of workers expect their retirement to last ten years or less. Another 15% believe it will last 11 to 19 years. In reality, half of the men living to age 65 can expect to be alive at age 82. Half of the women reaching age 65 will live to age 86. Imagine how much you will need to live on if you join the increasing number of Americans who live to be 100.

LONGEVITY FACTORS

Here are some factors that affect longevity:
- Ability to deal with stress;
- Family history and genes;
- Exercise;
- Eating habits;
- Weight;
- Nutrition;
- Attitude.

THE HEALTH FACTOR

Even if you're putting much younger people to shame in the workout room, good health comes with no guarantees. Healthcare expenses can alter the amount you will need in retirement and medical problems can put a damper on all of your retirement dreams. The health of your spouse or life partner can also change the course of your retirement.

SURVEY SHOWS MANY DON'T PREPARE

The 1999 Retirement Confidence Survey, conducted by the Employee Benefit Research Institute (EBRI), found that 6% of people age 54 or older had saved nothing for retirement and 11% of the people in that age group had saved under $10,000.

INFLATION CAN ERODE SAVINGS

Even at a modest rate of inflation, maintaining your lifestyle may cost more each year. For example, even though you may not be driving back and forth to work each day, gas prices may continue to rise.

▼ IT'S NOT AS GOOD AS A GENIE, BUT...
A good retirement plan can help make your dreams come true much more effectively than just wishing for them.

WHAT LIFESTYLE DO YOU WANT?

Retirement lifestyles come with different price tags. Golfing every day or traveling to exotic places will cost a lot more than the retirement dreams of someone who only wants a satellite dish and a remote control. Part of managing your money in retirement is making key decisions about what your lifestyle will be. Here are several factors to consider.

WHERE DO YOU WANT TO LIVE?

Decide whether you want to stay in your present home for as long as possible or whether to live out your days somewhere else. Keep in mind that the place where you vacation every year isn't necessarily the best place to retire. Chances are, you've only visited that area during the most desirable time of year and haven't seen it during the off-season. If you plan to work part-time or volunteer, make sure those types of opportunities exist in the area you're considering.

THINGS TO KNOW

Planned communities aren't for everyone. You will usually find many restrictions on how you can use your property. Read the community's rules and regulations before buying.

WHAT DO YOU PLAN TO DO?

If you're only happy when you're working, retirement may be a terrible disappointment. Map out your idea of a perfect day. If you love to travel, think about where you want to go and how to control the cost of those trips. Write down a list of hobbies and activities you've always wanted to try. If you already have a hobby, think about turning it into a business. Opening a small business in retirement can help you make the transition from a full-time job. It can also provide tax breaks and bring in a little extra money.

If retirement hasn't been all it's cracked up to be so far, shift directions. Sit down with your spouse or life partner and plot your next moves. If you're in a rut, you can do something different today and head off in a new direction.

WHAT SIZE HOME DO YOU WANT?

Perhaps, you like the city where you're living now, but your home is too big or those steps to the second floor seem to get steeper each year. Maybe, it's time to downsize to a smaller one-story house. The Taxpayer Relief Act of 1997 provides a great tax break for people who want to sell their primary dwelling. Here's why:

• A married couple, filing jointly, can make up to $500,000 on the sale of their primary dwelling and pay no federal income taxes;

• A single individual can make up to $250,000 on the sale of his or her primary dwelling without paying federal taxes on the gain.

The great part about this tax break is that you don't have to be 55 or older, as was once the case. It's no longer a once-in-a-lifetime tax break and you can take advantage of it every two years.

WORKSHEET ASSISTANCE

The American Savings Education Council offers a worksheet so you can estimate how much you need to save each year to reach your retirement goals. You can get a hard copy by calling 202-775-9130 or visiting its website at www.asec.org.

1 Explore work opportunities before deciding where to live. The retirement location you're considering may not lend itself to a business of that kind and jobs in your field may not be available.

2 If you have a life partner be sure to discuss your life visions and try to find common ground where both your dreams can be accommodated.

CHARTING YOUR FINANCIAL FUTURE

*I*t's not too late to be financially secure or to improve your financial situation. No matter what your current situation, there are certain steps to consider taking if you haven't already done so.

DIFFERENT GOALS FOR DIFFERENT PEOPLE

Even when you're retired, you have financial goals. Nearly every retiree's goals are different. Based on your vision of your future, consider the specific goals you want to set. For example, you may want to:

- Spend all of the money you have by the time you die;
- Live frugally and build an estate for your children, a friend, or a charity;
- Pay for a grandchild's education;
- Donate money annually.

Retirees also differ in one other important respect. Some have saved, invested, and planned well for retirement; others haven't. Even people who earned similar amounts during their lifetime and had similar family obligations may have extremely different amounts of money to manage in retirement. Retirees do, however, have at least one thing in common. They all want to be financially secure.

SET PRIORITIES

Even though priorities differ among retirees, everyone must decide what's important to them. Some rank gourmet dining as a priority, while others are content with a takeout cheeseburger. Some want to travel the world, while others are content with the comfort of their living room. Set your priorities and manage your money accordingly.

Your priorities in retirement can be compatible with your money management strategy. If you like traveling extensively, having a big expensive home may not be as important, which means you can downsize. If being charitable is a priority, volunteer your time in lieu of money gifts.

UNDERSTAND THE RISKS

Strategies for managing your money rely heavily on understanding and feeling comfortable with risks. Every investment carries some kind of risk. Even failing to invest is risky because you could well lose purchasing power every year to inflation. Most of all, no investment is worth having if you worry about it constantly. Make sure you're fully aware of your ability to deal with the fluctuations in value that come with higher-risk investments.

DIVERSIFY YOUR ASSETS

There are no guarantees when it comes to investing. Not many of us can predict the next hot sector of the economy or which stock will go through the roof. You can, however, couch your bets by having a good mix of investments. Most retirees should consider a diversified portfolio consisting of stocks, bonds, real estate, and cash.

▼ GET ALL YOUR DUCKS IN A ROW
You need to make certain arrangements to have a comfortable retirement. Now is the time to be making these plans.

3 Retirement gives you a lot of time to sit on your hands and do nothing if you choose. Plot your course and start moving toward the goals you've established.

SEE A LAWYER ABOUT ESTATE PLANNING

Retirees can differ enormously in their approach to preparing for death. Some don't want to deal with death or even discuss it. Others deal with every detail from picking a burial plot to selecting a casket. At a minimum, every adult needs a will. Even if you don't view yourself as wealthy, estate planning can be beneficial. It may also make sense to have a lawyer prepare other legal documents such as powers of attorney or a living trust.

LEGAL PREPARATIONS

P*rotecting what you have is more than just an investment strategy. It also means taking the legal steps necessary to protect your assets in case you die or can no longer care for yourself. Depending upon what state you're in, these documents should be considered.*

WILLS

No matter where you live or how much you have, you should consider having a will to ensure that your possessions are distributed to the people you designate. A will can make certain that your wishes, not the laws of the state, will govern the distribution of your property. A will can also determine who will care for your younger children, including any with special needs, assuming the other parent is unavailable.

Living will. This legal document is an offshoot of the will most of us consider. It permits you to state your wishes regarding life and death healthcare decisions, such as withholding or withdrawing life-sustaining treatment in certain circumstances.

TRUSTS

Most trusts are *living trusts*. A living trust is much like a will, but has one distinct advantage. Your assets go directly to your heirs without going through probate, which is the legal process for settling an estate. Living trusts are also more private than probate.

Irrevocable. You can create an irrevocable living trust where the assets in the trust can't be retrieved by you.

Revocable. This more common type of trust allows you to change your mind about the assets in the trust or the beneficiary of the trust. Keep in mind, however, that the property in a revocable living trust is still part of your estate.

Last Will & Testament

Be it known that I, _____, a resident of _____, County of _____, in the state of _____, being of sound mind, do make and declare this to be my Last Will and Testament expressly revoking all my prior Wills and Codicils at any time made.

DON'T LEAVE RELATIVES IN THE DARK

Life will be easier for yourself and loved ones if you keep a list with at least these items on it:

- The names, addresses, and phone numbers of all financial, legal, and other advisors;
- All account names, numbers, and locations of your investments;
- All of your creditors;
- The location of your will and the name of your executor;
- Safe deposit boxes and where they're located.

POWERS OF ATTORNEY

There are three basic kinds of legal documents called powers of attorney.

Power of attorney. With this, you authorize another person or organization to act on your behalf in a variety of legal and financial situations. It's no longer valid if you die or become incapacitated.

You can limit the time to a week or even a day and also limit its powers to a particular purpose, such as the power to sign a specific contract.

Durable power of attorney. This gives the person you designate the authority to manage your affairs if you become incapacitated.

Durable power of attorney for healthcare. This is a healthcare proxy which designates the named individual or individuals to make medical decisions on your behalf should you no longer be able to do so.

- Even if your estate is small, talk with a CPA or a tax attorney about income tax issues that arise on inherited IRAs, 401(k)s, and other retirement accounts. Even though your estate may not be subject to estate taxes, your beneficiaries may still have to pay income taxes.

- No matter how healthy you are, it's important to discuss your estate with an experienced attorney who understands the nuances of the legal documents discussed here. You also need to have adequate health insurance to cover the rising cost of medical treatment. Along with Medicare, a Medicare supplemental policy and long-term care insurance are worth considering.

- Make sure you have a copy of beneficiary designations for your retirement savings plans. These designations, not your will, control who gets your 401(k), IRA, or some other retirement accounts. The assets in these accounts pass directly to the beneficiary without going through probate, unless you name your estate as the beneficiary. To avoid the wrong people getting your money, take these steps.

- Find out who your beneficiary is on every account. Review those designations in conjunction with your will and your overall plan for distributing your property.

- Name a contingent beneficiary or beneficiaries in case the primary beneficiary dies.

- Keep a record of these designations with all of your other important papers, not stuffed in a drawer.

13

UNDERSTANDING RISKS

A s you attempt to protect what you have, generate income, and increase your assets, you will be faced with investment risks. Learning how to cope with them will increase your chances of successfully managing your money in retirement. Here are the major risks you face.

INFLATION RISK

You can have a lot of money, but it's not going to mean much if the necessities of life cost more each day. Whether it's groceries, gas, or the cost of medical care, it's difficult to cope with rising prices. Inflation can cause those prices to spiral upward and will result in the loss of purchasing power. If your investments don't keep pace with inflation, your income isn't going to be adequate.

LIQUIDITY RISK

Any investment that fluctuates in value can pose a threat to the investor who needs cash at a particular time. There's a distinct risk that you may need to liquidate the investment at the worst possible time.

INTEREST RATE RISK

Any fixed income investment is subject to interest rate risk. This is the risk that interest rates will rise and cause some fixed income investments, such as bonds, to lose value.

Many people don't understand that, like stocks, bonds can lose value as market conditions change. Typically, when interest rates rise, many bonds will drop in value (because newly issued bonds with the same qualities will carry higher interest, and therefore, be more attractive to investors).

In short, there is an inverse relationship between interest rates and bond values. When interest rates rise, bond prices go down. When interest rates go down, bond prices rise. A bond with a higher interest rate than the current available rates will usually be more valuable.

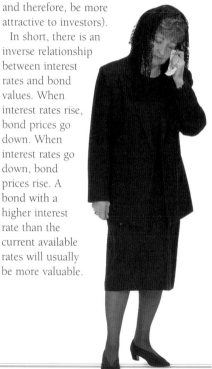

INDUSTRY RISK

An industry slowdown or problem can undermine what appears to be a solid investment. When there's a large verdict against cigarette manufacturers, tobacco industry stocks are hurt. In the early 1990s, Congress passed a luxury tax and the boating industry suffered severe economic problems. In most industries, there will be economic booms and busts.

The trade-off for taking risks is a higher rate of return. You will usually need to take more risks to achieve a greater rate of return. But by doing so, you risk losing part of your investment, losing income, and losing some or all of your assets.

THE RISK OF OUTLIVING YOUR MONEY

There are several reasons why you may outlive your money and it's not just from living too long.

- Your investments don't keep up with inflation;
- You withdraw too much;
- You don't invest wisely;
- You don't have a pension that pays income for life.

4 Every investment may have one, some, or all of the risks mentioned here.

CREDIT RISK

When you buy fixed income securities, you're lending money to a borrower. Credit risk is the likelihood that you will be paid back money you've lent in a timely fashion. The creditworthiness of that borrower (the credit *quality* of that borrower) determines the level of risk you're taking.

Generally, *issuers* (the ones who borrow your money) with the highest credit risk pay the highest interest rates in order to attract investors. Issuers with the lowest credit risk tend to pay the lowest interest rates because their safety tends to attract investors. Government bonds have almost no credit risk, while junk bonds may have a high risk that the borrower will default on its obligation.

MARKET RISK

Almost every investment has market risk and may lose value when faced with adverse economic conditions. The economic climate can affect even the bluest of blue-chip stocks, let alone a high-tech company or a start-up firm. Retirees must be aware of the market risk as they structure a portfolio for their retirement years.

DESIGN A STRATEGY

In order to achieve your financial goals, you have to make the most of the assets you have. Here are some ways to effectively manage your assets.

THREE MAIN STRATEGIES

Retirees are not a homogenous group. Just as your goals may be different than the goals of others, your strategies for achieving those goals can also be different. There are, however, three general strategies to consider. Your own may involve one strategy or a combination of strategies:

1 Live on your income without tapping principal;

1 Maximize your income, even if it exhausts principal;

1 Grow your principal as much as you possibly can.

IT'S A FACT

According to EBRI, the median 401(k) account balance in 1998 was $13,038.

PROTECT WHAT YOU HAVE

As a retiree, protecting your assets is extremely important. You're no longer at a job where you make more money each year. Instead of a paycheck, you depend upon the assets you've built up over the years. It's your job to make sure they're still working for you years from now.

When you're focused on protecting your money, the safety of an investment should be your most important consideration. Many retirees sacrifice their rate of return in order to have a very safe investment. What many overlook, however, is that their "safe" investments don't earn enough to keep up with inflation. In effect, they end up losing money anyway.

5 There are mutual funds that are designed specifically to blend more than one strategy for people who don't have cut-and-dried goals.

6 Don't wait until it's too late in the year to make tax maneuvers. Consider your tax situation before year-end to see what steps to take.

OVERLAPPING STRATEGIES

Although your focus may be on safety, income, or growth, a particular investment may have objectives that overlap. Sometimes, retirees may need to settle for something less than absolute safety to increase income. There are investments that can strike a balance between safety and income. Furthermore, there are strategies you can implement to reduce your investment risks. Talk to a financial professional, if you have questions you can't answer.

EARN INCOME FROM WHAT YOU HAVE

The assets you have can be used to generate income. You're in charge of earning as much income as you can without putting them in jeopardy.

Retirees usually focus on income more than growth. They gravitate to income investments such as bonds, certificates of deposit (CD's), and Treasury bills. Bonds are loans or debt issued by corporations or government entities to raise money. The issuer of a bond agrees to pay bondholders a specified amount of interest and to repay the principal at maturity (the end of the loan).

GROW MORE MONEY

Since retirement may last 20 years or longer, you probably still need to invest for growth. Otherwise, the income that seems sufficient today may no longer be adequate to carry you through an unpredictable number of years living your lifestyle. Younger retirees in particular should seriously consider investing for growth. Consequently, a retiree's portfolio should include individual stocks and mutual funds. Investing for growth is less risky when you have a long time horizon, meaning you won't need the money for at least five years.

PROTECTING WHAT YOU HAVE

There's one sure way to protect your assets in retirement: spend less than you're earning. Also make sure your investments don't give you a false sense of security.

INVESTING FOR PROTECTION

No strategy will guard against all risks, but buying a mix of investments (diversifying) can help protect against many downturns in the economy.

REAL ESTATE

Real estate has historically guarded well against inflation. When inflation has risen, real estate has typically increased in value, outpacing the inflation rate.

You can invest in real estate and still keep your money close to home by paying down your mortgage ahead of schedule. This will increase the equity in your home, which has two positive effects:

- You will increase the cash you keep if you eventually sell the home and pay off your loan;
- You increase the amount you could borrow on a home equity loan or similar loan. Be careful, though, with some loans such as negative amortization loans, which have low payments but raise the amount you end up owing.

I BONDS

I bonds are new Treasury bonds that offer protection against inflation. The return on the bond is linked to an inflation index. Here's how an I bond works:

Assigned rate. There's a fixed rate assigned at purchase that remains with the bond for life. A portion of the bond's earnings are tied to the Consumer Price Index.

Face value price. Unlike the older series E and series EE bonds, the I bond is purchased at face value. Upon redemption, the bond pays the face value of the bond, plus all of the interest that has accrued.

Increasing value. The I bond increases in value monthly and interest is compounded semi-annually.

Minimum holding. The bond must be held for at least six months before cashing. If you don't hold it for five years, you will lose three months' worth of interest.

7 Although the interest on I bonds is taxable, it's usually exempt from state and local taxes.

CASH EQUIVALENTS

The investment industry provides a number of investments designed to protect your money as their top priority. Securities in an asset class called *cash equivalents* help you protect your money while earning a small amount of income at the same time. They're called cash equivalents because they're designed to be almost as safe as cash—and to be available to convert to cash as soon as you make the demand.

Cash equivalents are securities that let you keep your money close and safe by lending it for very short periods (less than a year) to borrowers with reliable reputations. Money market funds are an example of a cash equivalent and are similar to savings accounts except that your money is pooled with other customers into one large sum. The money is then loaned to businesses for a short time, usually for a week or less and sometimes overnight.

Money market funds are considered one of the safest types of investments. The interest earned is shared by all shareholders minus a small fee the fund takes for its efforts. Bank money market funds are federally insured (FDIC). Money market *mutual* funds usually come with private insurance.

TRUSTS

A trust is a legal arrangement in which you hold property for the benefit of others (called beneficiaries). Trusts can be used to effectively carry out your wishes while you're alive, or after your death.

LIVING TRUSTS

Living trusts are created during your lifetime. They have three major benefits:

- They let you avoid the expense of probate;
- Unlike wills, trusts are not public documents, so how you distribute your property remains private;
- You're virtually assured that your assets will be handled according to your wishes if you become incapacitated. The trustee you name will manage your legal and financial affairs during your lifetime if you're incapable of doing so.

The living trust, in particular, is increasingly used by retirees of all income levels to manage their assets during their lifetime and to settle their affairs at death. Living trusts can either be revocable or irrevocable.

Revocable living trusts. If you live in an area where there is a high percentage of older people, you may hear ads extolling the benefits of revocable living trusts. Revocable living trusts can ease some of the problems associated with dying, but you should be aware of their limitations:

- Because they're revocable, the property is still part of your estate and may be subject to estate taxes;
- Because the assets in the trust remain your property, you will still lose some or all of those assets if you're attempting to qualify for Medicaid to pay for long-term care;
- If not drafted correctly, living trusts can create legal problems—not reduce them;
- All of your real and personal property must be made part of one or more living trusts or probate may still be necessary.

8 You can hold stock, bond, or mutual fund investment accounts in a trust. Check with an estate planning advisor.

9 It's a misconception that trusts are only for the wealthy. There are trusts for virtually anyone.

TESTAMENTARY TRUSTS

The testamentary trust is established in your will and doesn't go into effect until your death. The trust takes control of your assets at death and distributes them as you've directed. There are several reasons to create a testamentary trust:

- It offers protection for your children and other beneficiaries;
- It allows you to provide for children with special needs or offspring from a previous marriage;
- It can be used to assure a steady income for your spouse;
- It can control how the beneficiary uses income from the trust after your death.

Because your will can be torn up at any time, the testamentary trust is revocable.

IRREVOCABLE LIFE INSURANCE TRUSTS

If you have a large life insurance policy, this trust will let you avoid having the proceeds included in your estate.

CHARITABLE TRUSTS

Charitable trusts are set up to benefit a qualified charity. The trust may also result in tax benefits for you, as well as an income stream.

A charitable *lead* trust pays income to the charity for a specified period of time. After that time, the property in the trust is distributed to your beneficiaries.

A charitable *remainder* trust is funded with property that eventually goes to the charity. In the interim, the income goes to you or your beneficiaries.

BYPASS TRUST

The bypass trust is designed to keep you from wasting your *unified tax credit*. Upon your death, the $675,000 in your estate that's exempt from taxes (the credit) can be deposited in the bypass trust. Your spouse then receives the income from the trust for life. Even though your spouse receives income from the trust, it's not considered part of your spouse's estate. As a result, s/he will continue to have a $675,000 exemption from estate taxes.

DISCOUNTS

*L*ife has changed a great deal since you went to the movies as a youngster and got a discount for being under a certain age. (Movies have changed a great deal as well.) Today, discounts range from purchases on the Internet to a free meal on your birthday.

SENIOR-ORIENTED DISCOUNTS

The good news about getting older is that your age entitles you to discounts on food, merchandise, and services. Don't be embarrassed to admit your age and ask for your discount. Here are a few you might find:

- The American Association of Retired Persons (AARP) offers an inexpensive membership to people who are 50 or older. Your AARP card will get you discounts on hotels, travel, merchandise, and services;
- The airlines offer travel discounts to seniors;
- Many clothing stores and other merchants offer discounts to seniors on specified days of the week;
- Some fast food franchises give free beverages to seniors or a discount on the food purchased;

- In certain cities, seniors are entitled to free or reduced rates on public transportation during certain hours. There are often programs that provide taxi cab service to senior citizens;
- Seniors can get discounts on movies, museums, and other forms of entertainment. They can also get reduced prices on haircuts and other services by showing proof of age;
- When you're traveling by car from state to state, stop in the welcome center at the border. You will find discount coupons for lodging, attractions, activities, and restaurants.

◀ BE RESOURCEFUL
You can find all kinds of discounts at all sorts of different places. Don't be afraid to ask if there's a senior discount. You may be pleasantly surprised.

ORGANIZATIONS TO JOIN THAT OFFER DISCOUNTS

There are many organizations that offer discounts to their members. These are a few of them:

- Motor clubs have more benefits than just jump starting your car on a winter day. Most clubs offer discounts on hotels, travel, and attractions. You might even get discounted tickets to concerts and sporting events. You will also get reduced prices on services for your car;

- Entertainment books are sold in most major cities by charitable organizations. They offer two-for-one dining at the better restaurants, as well as fast food franchises. You get discounts on hotels, rental cars, stores, golf courses, dry cleaning, and an assortment of other services;

- Many credit cards offer cash back, airline points, discounts on purchases, and other incentives for using their card. As long as you pay your balance in full each month and don't incur a finance charge, these credit card perks are attractive;

- Buy a membership to a warehouse club. You're able to purchase many items at a discount just by belonging to one.

10 To possibly cut costs of foreign travel, check the exchange rate of the U.S. dollar in relation to the currency of the country you're visiting.

11 Always compare the prices and discounts before paying the membership fee at price clubs.

DISCOUNTS FOR ANYONE

Younger retirees don't have to feel bad because they're not old enough to qualify for some discounts. There are other discounts available that aren't age related:

- Many restaurants offer early-bird dinners to patrons who eat before a certain time. You will sometimes find special prices if you eat out on a weekday. These deals won't be available on weekends when the restaurant is typically more crowded;

- Get out those scissors and start cutting. You can find coupons in the newspaper, on the Internet, and in direct mailings from merchants in your area;

- Many businesses offer a discount for paying cash.

CUTTING BACK ON EXPENSES

Maybe, you look back fondly on the days when you had an expense account. Now all of those lunches and trips come out of your own pocket. But you can enjoy a nice lifestyle on a modest budget.

12 Miscellaneous expenses are often the problem. Take a week and write down every penny you spend. You will be surprised by how much you're spending.

EXAMINING LIVING EXPENSES

Initially, you need to determine how much your lifestyle is costing now. Take a look at these expenses and how much you're spending on a monthly basis:

- Mortgage or rent;
- Property taxes;
- Home maintenance and upkeep;
- Food;
- Clothing;
- Utilities;
- Auto-related expenses (gas, tolls, repairs, etc.);
- Insurance (auto, homeowners, health, life);
- Medical and dental expenses;
- Entertainment;
- Travel;
- Loans and credit card debt;
- Miscellaneous expenses.

WHEN YOUR BUDGET ISN'T WORKING

Retirees often find they're spending more in retirement than they projected. A miscalculation of 10% is to be expected. Here are some reasons why this happens. They have:

- More time to spend money and shop;
- More leisure time and will be involved in more activities that cost money;
- More time to travel;
- A greater tendency to splurge.

24

STEPS TO TAKE IF YOU'RE OVER YOUR BUDGET

If you're over budget, you risk running out of money and may need to pull in the reigns right away. Some people consider taking these steps.

Luxuries/necessities. Distinguish between items you must buy and things it would be nice to own.

Stop credit cards. Put away your credit cards to help curb impulse spending. Only carry your credit cards for a planned purchase.

Avoid ATM withdrawals. Decide how much cash you need and don't spend a penny more.

Buy right. With the right planning, you can buy most of the things you want at a more reasonable price. Thoroughly investigating each purchase can help you get the best value or you may decide that a purchase isn't worth the money.

Overspending. Don't overspend in one budget area without cutting corners in another. If you take an expensive trip, you may want to cut corners by eating out less often or by waiting for movies to come to the bargain theater.

Move or sell something. It may be time to move to a smaller house or sell that second car.

Coordinate. Make sure you and your life partner (if you have one) are on the same page when it comes to spending. Try to agree on a budget that both of you can live with without feeling deprived.

EXPENSES NO MORE

In retirement, some expenses are likely to go up, while others are likely to come down. Here are some expenses that may go away:

- Mortgage;
- Commuting costs, unless you get a part-time job;
- Work-related expenses like lunches out or clothing;
- Financial responsibility for children.

But there may also be expenses that go up, such as:

- Healthcare;
- A second home;
- Travel;
- Entertainment.

13 Leave room in your budget for unexpected expenses. You never know when the furnace will stop or your car will need an expensive repair.

25

LONG-TERM CARE INSURANCE

*W*hen you're managing money in retirement, a devastating illness can spoil all of your plans. Sometimes, it's not just an illness that can cause you personal and economic problems.

WHY HAVE IT

Long-term care is ongoing care that assists you with the activities of daily living. There are three reasons why long-term care may become necessary:

- Aging;
- Accident;
- Illness.

A person should consider buying a long-term care policy:

- To preserve financial independence;
- To protect your family from enormous long-term care costs;
- To avoid becoming a burden on your family and friends;
- To conserve your estate and preserve your spouse's income;
- To avoid Medicaid;
- To increase your chances of receiving your preferred choice of long-term care.

WHAT IT CAN COST

If long-term care becomes necessary, get ready for a phenomenal bill. According to the MetLife Mature Market Institute, nursing home care costs an average of $153 per day. The average stay is 2 1/2 years and $139,000. If you live in Manhattan, a private room can cost $295 per day. That's over $100,000 per year. The cost of home healthcare could easily be $36,000 per year or more if there are special medical problems.

IT'S A FACT

According to the American Council of Life Insurance less than 10 percent of the nation's elderly population have purchased long-term care insurance.

 14 Long-term care insurance may be more important to women because they are more likely to outlive men and need nursing home care.

WHO QUALIFIES

The activities of daily living (ADLs) are the typical standard in a long-term care policy to determine whether the insured qualifies for benefits. There are six ADLs usually specified in a long-term care policy:

- Eating;
- Bathing;
- Toileting;
- Dressing;
- Continence (the ability to control bowel and bladder function);
- Transferring from bed to chair or wheelchair.

WHO PAYS FOR IT

Unfortunately, Medicare and Medicare supplements don't normally cover long-term care. Medicare will only cover skilled nursing care or skilled rehabilitation services. Most long-term care is custodial, not skilled. Medicare supplemental policies (aka Medigap policies) only fill in the gaps and provide little coverage for long-term care expenses. Medicaid pays for nursing home care, but you risk losing most of your assets in order to qualify. The long-term care policy was designed to cover these expenses.

RECENT STUDY

A recent study conducted by the American Council of Life Insurers projects that long-term care expenses will quadruple by 2030. Here are recent costs and future estimates:

- Adult day care averages $12,981 per year. It will cost an average of $56,100 a year in 2030;
- Home healthcare averages $15,743 a year. It will cost $68,000 per year in 2030;
- A year in an assisted living facility averages $25,300 per year. In 2030, it's projected to be $109,300 a year;
- Nursing home care averages $44,100 per year and will cost $190,600 in 2030.

GENERATING INCOME

No matter what your situation, you can generate more income and improve your finances. Even if buying a yacht is out of reach, you can enhance your lifestyle and have more things you want.

SOCIAL SECURITY

Social Security benefits encompass much more than just retirement checks. There are five major categories of benefits financed by Social Security taxes.

DISABILITY

Social Security protects people of any age who become disabled. To be considered disabled, you must have a severe physical or mental impairment. Spouses, ex-spouses, and children are protected even if they have no work record of their own. When the parent retires, the disabled child receives 50 percent of the parent's full retirement benefit. After the parent dies, the disability benefit is 75 percent.

MEDICARE

Approximately 39 million people are covered by Medicare. This federal medical insurance program covers people over age 65 and certain disabled individuals. Medicare consists of Part A which pays for inpatient hospital care, skilled nursing care and other services. Medicare Part B pays for doctor's fees, and outpatient hospital visits, as well as other services and supplies.

IT'S A FACT

The Social Security trust fund has enough assets to cover checks until the year 2037.

RETIREMENT BENEFITS

Even though the age to receive full retirement benefits is rising, you can still collect at age 62. Unfortunately, your benefit check will be a lot less. People who delay receiving Social Security benefits until after their official retirement age receive a larger check when they do retire. Divorced men and women can collect retirement benefits under their former spouse's Social Security record if that person's earnings are higher. There are three tests to qualify. You must be:

- At least 62. (The age is 60 if your spouse or former spouse is deceased.);
- Unmarried;
- We're married to your former spouse for at least 10 years.

You can receive benefits even if your former spouse is still working and has remarried. A previous requirement that the former spouse be retired has been eliminated. Otherwise, the former spouse might continue working in order to prevent the "ex" from drawing benefits.

FAMILY BENEFITS

If you're found to be eligible for retirement or disability benefits, your spouse, ex-spouse, and children are protected too.

SURVIVORS BENEFITS

If you earned enough credits during your work years, Social Security also protects members of your family who survive you. The rules can be complicated. Contact the Social Security Administration or check their website at www.ssa.gov.

SS AND INFLATION

Even though Social Security recipients get a raise every year, these increases won't necessarily keep pace with inflation. Though Social Security beneficiaries receive a cost-of-living adjustment based upon the Consumer Price Index, that small increase won't do much to combat inflation. Here are some past adjustments.

1996 2.6%
1997 2.9%
1998 2.1%
1999 1.3%
2000 2.4%
2001 3.4%

WORKING

U*ntil recently, a large number of retirees were punished for working. The Senior Citizens' Freedom to Work Act of 2000 makes it possible for many Social Security beneficiaries to earn as much as they want without reducing their benefits.*

THE IMPACT OF WORK ON BENEFITS

Prior to the passage of the new law, you had to wait until age 70 to earn an unlimited amount without any impact on your Social Security check. The new law changed age 70 to the retirement age.

Retirement age isn't necessarily 65 and may be as old as 67. It's still 65 if you reach that age prior to January 1, 2003.

If you're younger than the retirement age and collecting Social Security benefits, you will still be penalized for working. $1 will be deducted from your Social Security check for every $2 you earn over $10,800.

OFFICIAL RETIREMENT AGE

Birth Year	Retirement Age
1937 or before	65
1938	65 and 2 months
1939	65 and 4 months
1940	65 and 6 months
1941	65 and 8 months
1942	65 and 10 months
1943-1954	66
1955	66 and 2 months
1956	66 and 4 months
1957	66 and 6 months
1958	66 and 8 months
1959	66 and 10 months
1960 or later	67

BRIDGE WORK

According to EBRI, many older Americans are leaving the work force, opting for *bridge jobs* before they withdraw completely from work. Bridge jobs are part-time or short-term jobs either in a new line of work or in the same field as a previous career. An EBRI study found that 1/3 to 1/2 of older Americans will hold a bridge job before permanently leaving work.

15 Good reasons for working in retirement include extra money, keeping active, preventing boredom, staying sharp, and staying sociable.

TURNING A HOBBY INTO A BUSINESS

One reason why people retire is that they have dreams of devoting more time to hobbies and activities they love. Some hobbies have the potential to earn money if you turn them into a business. You need to ask yourself these questions before turning a hobby into a business:

- Will I enjoy the hobby as much if I'm working at it full-time?
- Will the business prevent me from enjoying my other retirement activities?
- How much money will it take to start the business?
- Will I risk any of my retirement assets to finance the business?
- How easy is it to start a business of this kind?
- What insurance do I need for this business?

STARTING SMALL AND HOME BUSINESSES

A small business, especially one you operate out of your home, offers numerous tax breaks. Of course, the IRS must be convinced that you earnestly want to make a go of the business and aren't still treating it as a hobby. Here are some of the possible tax breaks:

- You can write off a portion of your home-related expenses such as utilities;
- Your health insurance premiums may be deductible;
- Certain expenses like buying a computer may be deductible;
- There will be opportunities for business-related travel;
- Certain books you buy and memberships will be deductible;
- Certain entertainment expenses may be partially deductible.

31

RETIREMENT PLAN WITHDRAWALS

Now that it's time to consider tapping into your retirement plans, be sure you understand the sometimes complex rules that must be followed.

CONSIDER THE TAXES

Your employer-sponsored account, along with your IRAs, may turn out to be your biggest source of income in retirement. But one problem may be how to effectively take out money from your IRAs and 401(k)s. In terms of tax considerations, there are two types of withdrawals.

Taxable. These are withdrawals on which you still owe taxes. Qualified withdrawals from a traditional IRA and a 401(k) are taxable. If you take too much, you will find yourself in a higher tax bracket.

Tax-free. These are withdrawals on which you don't owe taxes. Qualified withdrawals from a Roth IRA aren't taxable. If all of your withdrawals come from a Roth IRA, you will be in good shape at tax time.

IRA TO ROTH

Ask your tax advisor if it makes sense to convert your traditional IRA—or to transfer some money—to a Roth IRA. You will pay taxes at the time of conversion or transfer, but sometimes it pays off in the long run.

IRA WITHDRAWALS

Once you reach the age of 59 1/2, you can withdraw the contributions you've made, as well as the money earned, without paying the 10% penalty for early withdrawals. If you want, however, to move your IRA, you may run into a tax problem. Here are two possible scenarios and how to avoid taxation.

Direct transfers. You can transfer an IRA directly from one trustee or custodian to another without causing a tax problem. The IRS places no limits on the number of times you can transfer an IRA each year.

Rollovers. Sometimes, people decide to take a distribution from their IRA as cash instead of having the funds transferred directly by the financial institution to another IRA. By doing so, they risk paying taxes and penalties for a premature withdrawal. To avoid those taxes and penalties, the distribution or payout must be rolled over to another IRA in 60 days or less.

16 Unlike transfers, you're only permitted one rollover in a 12-month period.

ROTH IRA WITHDRAWALS

The key feature of Roth IRAs is that all of your distributions are tax-free—as long as you play by the rules. There are two requirements for taking these tax-free distributions:

● The IRA must have been open for at least five years;

● You must be at least 59 1/2.

Unlike traditional IRAs, there are no minimum withdrawal requirements at age 70 1/2. If you wish, you can keep as much money as you want in the account as long as you want it to keep growing.

 17 You can't transfer a 401(k) to a Roth IRA. Qualified withdrawals from Roth IRAs are tax-free, while those from 401(k)s are taxable.

MANDATORY WITHDRAWALS FROM A TRADITIONAL IRA

If you don't need the money from your traditional IRA, you can wait until you reach age 70 1/2 to begin withdrawals from the account.

Timing. You must make your first withdrawal by age 70 1/2 or April 1 of the following year at the latest. Think twice about waiting until April, because you will still have to make your second withdrawal by December 31 of that same year. As a result, you will have two withdrawals in the same year, which could throw you into a higher tax bracket.

Amount. You must withdraw the correct amount or face penalties. Failing to make the appropriate mandatory withdrawal could create penalties of 50% of the amount that should have been withdrawn.

Your withdrawal is based upon your life expectancy, or the joint life expectancy of you and your beneficiary. The younger the beneficiary, the smaller the amount of your mandatory withdrawal. There are limits, however, on how young that beneficiary may be. Consult a tax advisor.

INCOME FROM EMPLOYER PLANS

E *ven if you hated your job and your employer, you will hopefully have one great keepsake—your retirement savings plan. If you contributed regularly, invested well, and your employer made a generous match, you may have a lot of money. The problem is how to withdraw it without causing yourself a major tax problem. Here are three options.*

18 401(k)s are *portable.* This means that you can take your retirement savings with you when you leave a job.

TAKE A LUMP-SUM DISTRIBUTION

If you're at least 59 1/2 or 55 and no longer working, you can withdraw your entire 401(k) without incurring the 10 percent tax penalty. But assuming it's a large account, you're likely to put yourself in a higher tax bracket.

PART-TIME MAY BE ENOUGH

If you decide to work part-time in retirement, see if you're eligible to contribute to the company's 401(k) plan. Even if you don't stay long enough for the employer's contribution to vest, you will have another tax-sheltered retirement account to fall back on.

Mutual Fund Retirement Assets by Type of Fund, 1999
(billions of dollars)

	Equity		Bond	Hybrid	Money Market	Total
	Domestic	Foreign				
IRAs	$762	$125	$100	$97	$140	$1,222
401(k)	553	64	38	73	49	777
403(b) Plans	230	18	8	12	13	281
Other Employer-Sponsored Plans	113	18	32	12	18	192
Total	**$1,658**	**$224**	**$177**	**$194**	**$219**	**$2,472**

Note: Components may not add up exactly to the totals due to rounding.
Source: Mutual Fund Factbook, Investment Company Institute.

LEAVE THE MONEY IN THE PLAN

If you're comfortable with the investment options in the 401(k), you may want to keep your funds there for the foreseeable future. If your balance is below $5,000, the employer isn't obligated to offer this option.

Make sure you're not keeping too much money in your employer's stock. Some employers are now offering a trading option as part of 401(k)s. Much like a self-directed brokerage account, you can buy or sell stocks or select mutual funds from outside the standard list of investment choices.

 19 Make certain there are no additional fees for retirees. Fees can have a significant impact over the years on your return on investment.

ROLL THE MONEY OVER INTO AN IRA

To avoid any tax problems, you can have the money in your 401(k) transferred directly into an IRA at a bank, brokerage firm, or mutual fund company. If the proceeds of your 401(k) are sent directly to you, you only have 60 days (including weekends and holidays) to roll over the full amount into an IRA. Complicating that rollover is the fact that your employer must withhold 20 percent of the 401(k) for income taxes. You must use your own money to make up the difference, so you can roll over the full amount.

Keep in mind that once you transfer your money to an IRA, you normally must wait until age 59 1/2 to get your money. When the money is in a 401(k), you must be age 55 or older to tap into it without the 10% penalty, as long as you're not working.

SOME TAX ISSUES

If Social Security benefits and part-time work aren't sufficient to support your lifestyle, you will need income from investments.

TAXES ON VARIOUS INVESTMENTS

Your money could go farther if you consider the impact of taxes. Although it's generally presumed that retirees are in a lower tax bracket, it doesn't always turn out that way.

Retirement plans. Withdrawals from IRAs, pensions, interest, capital gains, and dividends can throw you into a higher tax bracket. Even if your estate is small, talk with a CPA or a tax attorney about income tax issues that arise on inherited IRAs, 401(k)s, and other retirement accounts. Even though your estate may not be subject to estate taxes, your beneficiaries may still have to pay income taxes.

Social Security. Recipients have more to worry about than just the tax bracket. If you're married, filing a joint return, and your income is over $32,000, you may be required to pay taxes on up to 50% of your benefits. If you're single, the ceiling is $25,000. What's worse, if you're married with income over $44,000 ($34,000 for singles), you may be taxed on up to 85% of your benefits.

Municipal bonds. If you're in a high tax bracket during retirement, tax-free investments are worth considering.

These bonds pay less interest, but there's no federal tax on the income. Municipals are typically debt obligations of a state, city, school district, or other public entity. In some instances, the income will also be exempt from state and local taxes. Check to see if the tax break adequately compensates you for the lower interest rate.

Annuities. The payout on annuities helps your tax situation because some checks are considered a return of principal, not interest. There's also a tax break with annuities during the accumulation phase.

BREAKS FOR SENIORS

There are several tax rules that benefit senior citizens:

- You may not have to file a tax return if your income is below a certain threshold;
- You receive a higher standard deduction;
- There's a limited tax credit if you receive little or no Social Security benefits.

You have to be 65 or older to take advantage of most tax breaks.

HH BONDS

If you don't want to pay taxes on the interest accrued from Savings Bonds, consider exchanging Savings Bonds for the HH series. If you exchange a bond for an HH bond, you don't have to pay taxes on all the interest that has been deferred since its purchase. Instead, it all rolls over into the HH bond and won't be due until the HH bond is redeemed. With your new HH bond, you will only pay taxes on the interest it earns.

When interest is paid. Interest is paid every six months. To assure a monthly check, you can convert your bonds each month to HH bonds so each will reach the six-month mark at a different time.

How to exchange. You can't buy HH bonds with cash. They're only available in exchange for Series E, EE, Savings Notes, and Series H bonds that have reached final maturity. Since HH bonds are sold in $500 increments, the value of bonds you're exchanging won't exactly match what you're buying. Therefore, you're permitted to add money to reach the next $500 increment—or you can take money back and round down to the next lower $500 increment, but some or all of that money will be taxable.

TAX-QUALIFIED POLICIES

When you buy a tax-qualified long-term care policy, you are assured that the policy has certain features mandated by the Health Insurance Portability and Accountability Act of 1996 (HIPAA). Buying a tax-qualified policy also assures that some or all of your premium is tax-deductible. A tax-qualified policy will also have a benefit eligibility standard that is no more restrictive than the following:

- Due to disability or age, you are expected to be unable to do at least two of the six activities of daily living without substantial help for at least 90 days; or,
- You need substantial supervision to protect your health and safety because you're cognitively impaired.

TYPES OF FIXED INCOME

Y ou've probably heard fellow retirees complain, "I can't afford that. I'm on a fixed income." One reason your income is fixed is because you're depending upon fixed income investments to provide steady income.

VARIOUS STRATEGIES

There are several approaches to generating income from your investments. **Play it safe.** You can invest for safety even if it means earning a low rate of return, but you might not even keep up with inflation.

Earn income. You might focus on income investments and try to maximize the amounts you earn. Be aware that bonds differ in quality (credit risk). Generally, the lower the quality, the higher the interest, and the higher the quality, the lower the risk. You could lose principal, although only low-rated bonds generally present a considerable credit risk.

Income and growth. You might look for investments that offer income and some growth potential. Typically, these are stocks that pay solid dividends and represent companies with a solid business outlook.

Income and security. Preferred stocks offer ownership in a company with dividends secured by that company's assets. If a company is liquidated, preferred stockholders have preference in being repaid over common stockholders. In exchange for this security, you typically lose most of the growth potential of a common stock because preferred stock prices tend not to fluctuate much.

MONEY MARKET FUNDS

Money market funds are a safe and liquid investment. They invest in high quality short-term debt. Money market mutual funds are quite similar, but they aren't FDIC insured, even if you buy it through a bank.

CERTIFICATES OF DEPOSIT (CD'S)

A CD pays a fixed rate of return on funds deposited for a specified length of time. CD's are issued by banks, savings and loans, and credit unions. They are normally insured by the FDIC or the FSLIC and have a penalty for early withdrawal.

Choosing the maturity date of a CD is difficult, because you're never quite sure if you should lock in a higher rate for a longer timeframe. You will have more liquidity if you stagger the maturity dates of your CD's so they come due at regular intervals. When each CD matures, you can turn it into cash or buy a new CD. If you buy a new CD, the new interest rate may be lower or higher than the old CD. Accordingly, you may have less income generated by the new CD—or you may have more.

BONDS

A bond is actually a loan which investors make to a corporation or the government that pays a stated return over a specified period of time. When you think of a conservative way to generate income for retirement, most investors think of bonds.

Treasury bills. These are short-term government securities with maturity dates of no more than one year. They're also called T-bills. Treasury notes mature in one to ten years. Treasury bonds are longer-term securities of ten years or more.

If interest rates go up after buying them and you want to sell, you will be selling them at a discount from face value. If interest rates go down, you would be able to sell them at more than face value.

Corporate bonds. With these, you're lending money to a corporation. Because they're not backed by the full faith and credit of the government, they pay a higher interest rate than U.S. Treasury bonds. Corporate bonds differ greatly in quality. Lower quality bonds, sometimes called junk bonds, pay a higher rate, but pose a greater risk of default.

Zero coupon bonds. These are issued at a discount to their face value of $1,000. You receive no interest but you're paid the $1,000 at maturity. Even though you receive no interest payments, the IRS will tax you as if you did. This applies to corporate zero coupon bonds, but not zero municipal bonds, if you live in the state in which they were issued.

BONDS AREN'T RISK-FREE

Buying a bond sounds risk-free, but there are reasons why it isn't. Suppose you buy a $50,000 bond that pays 8% interest until it matures in 25 years. Here are some of the dangers:

- **You may want to sell the bond before it matures.** If investors can get more than 8% somewhere else, your bond isn't worth as much. You have to accept a lower price to make up for the fact that it pays less than the going rate of interest. If interest rates in general are lower than what your bond is paying, you will receive more than the face value of the bond;

- **There is a credit risk with certain bonds.** The entity responsible for paying you interest, as well as the principal at maturity, may run into financial problems;

- **You also risk losing ground to inflation.** In 25 years, that $50,000 will not have the same purchasing power as it does now. Time erodes the value of your principal. If the interest from bonds is your only income, your standard of living will suffer as consumer prices rise;

- **The bond may be callable.** This means the issuer can redeem it before maturity.

BOND MUTUAL FUNDS

L ike other kinds of mutual funds, bond funds pool money from many investors and create a diversified portfolio. The fund manager decides which bonds to buy and sell and when to buy and sell them. The parameters for these buy and sell decisions must be in compliance with the fund's investment objective, which can be found in its prospectus.

HOW THEY WORK

You can buy or sell shares in a bond mutual fund at any time. Depending upon where you buy the bond, you will either pay the net asset value (NAV) (directly from the fund) for each share or you will pay the NAV plus a commission (through your broker). NAV reflects the actual value of the bonds in the fund's portfolio. NAV is recalculated on a daily basis and may be higher or lower than the amount you paid per share.

Bond mutual funds are considered to be fixed income investments, but that doesn't mean the value of your fund shares won't go up and down. In fact, they often do.

On an ongoing basis, the fund manager will sell bonds at a gain or a loss in order to have the money to buy other bonds s/he finds more attractive. In addition, some bonds will mature (end). The cash returned to the fund by the bond issuer will be reinvested in other bonds at different interest rates and prices. Finally, if interest rates in general are going up, it is likely that the value of your shares will go down—and vice versa.

◀ EVERYBODY IN THE POOL

Mutual funds aren't limited to accepting money from investors in their own country. As long as they're able to open an account in the fund's country, virtually any investor from any country can pool their money in a mutual fund.

TYPES OF BOND MUTUAL FUNDS

There are numerous categories of bond mutual funds. Some bond mutual funds blend bonds of various types such as corporate and government bonds. Here are some of the major categories.

Corporate bond funds. These consist primarily of bonds issued by corporations, but they may also include U.S. Treasury bonds or other types of bonds.

High-yield bond funds. These invest in bonds issued by companies who are relatively risky borrowers, so they must offer to pay high interest rates to attract investors. These are sometimes called *junk bonds*.

Income funds. These invest in a mixture of corporate and government bonds and are designed to provide investors with a competitive interest rate.

Municipal bond funds. These feature bonds issued by states and municipalities. Generally, your income is exempt from federal income taxes. You will see several categories of municipal bond funds. For example, short-term municipal bond funds buy bonds that mature in a relatively short period of time.

U.S. government bond funds. These cover more than just Treasury bills. They invest in a variety of government obligations such as U.S. Treasury bonds, Ginnie Maes, and other government notes. Ginnie Mae funds invest in mortgages backed by the Government National Mortgage Association (GNMA). Though the mortgages are backed by the government, the shares in Ginnie Mae funds rise and fall in relation to interest rates.

BOND FUNDS VS. INDIVIDUAL BONDS

Here are some advantages of owning a bond fund:

- You can buy shares for a relatively small amount;
- You can arrange for the fund to send you a check each month;
- You can reduce your risk when purchasing high-yield junk bonds because of the diversification that comes with buying a mutual fund.

Here are some disadvantages of owning a bond fund:

- The annual expenses of the fund reduce your rate of return;
- With individual bonds, you can lock in an income stream. With a bond fund, your monthly income may fluctuate because of rising and falling interest rates.

20 Many banks sell bond mutual funds and annuities. Although you buy these products at a bank, they aren't federally (FDIC) insured.

41

ANNUITIES

Annuities can help assure that you won't outlive your income. For example, you can choose a payout option that creates a stream of income for your lifetime, as well as for a loved one.

WHAT THEY ARE

An annuity is a contract between you and an insurance company. Based upon the amount you pay in premiums, the insurance company pays out money to you on an agreed upon schedule. If you want payments to begin immediately, you might opt for an *immediate annuity*. Otherwise, you might buy a *deferred annuity*.

Annuities offer a tax-sheltered vehicle to invest for retirement and a way to guarantee an income for life, or in the alternative, a set amount of income for a specific number of years. As a general rule, you can't withdraw funds from the account before age 59 1/2. After that, you're only taxed on the earnings withdrawn.

> **21** Study bonus offers on fixed annuities that make it look like you're getting a higher than usual interest rate. The bonus rate may only be good for a limited time.

TWO MAIN TYPES

There are two main types:

Fixed. Fixed annuities guarantee that your investment will earn a fixed interest rate for a set period of time. The insurance company hopes to make more on the money invested than it will be required to pay you. There may also be mortality and expense charges deducted.

Variable. Variable annuities offer many investment options. Typically, you allocate the money invested in an annuity among a variety of mutual funds with different investment objectives. You control how your money is invested, not the insurer. If you're willing to take the risk and invest somewhat aggressively, the variable annuity can produce a higher rate of return than a fixed annuity.

The earnings in an annuity are sheltered from taxes until you begin making withdrawals. The fees and charges can affect the potential growth of the investment.

> **22** An annuity bought at a bank is not FDIC insured.

EVALUATING AN ANNUITY

Before buying, evaluate some of the main features.

Surrender charge. There's a surrender charge if you want to cash out of the annuity. This charge is the insurance company's way of recapturing the commission it paid to the salesperson. The amount is clearly stated in the annuity contract and differs from company to company. Usually, the surrender charge will go down each year until it completely disappears.

Withdrawals. The contract should allow for partial withdrawals. Typically, you can take out up to 10% of the accumulated cash value in a year. This can be useful if you need to tap the annuity during the years the surrender charge is in effect. In addition to the penalties imposed by the contract, taking money from an annuity may result in tax penalties.

As a general rule, if you withdraw money from an annuity prior to age 59 1/2, you will owe a 10% early withdrawal tax penalty. This applies to earnings, not the amount you deposited. Withdrawals are viewed as earnings first, however, not as principal. When you *annuitize* and begin taking a stream of income, your payments represent both earnings and principal, so you aren't taxed on the full amount.

Safety. There are independent rating services that examine the financial health of insurance companies, such as A.M. Best and Weiss Research.

▲ A STEADY SOURCE

The biggest attraction of an annuity is that it offers you a guaranteed, steady source of income that you can arrange to suit your individual life needs.

EXCHANGING ONE ANNUITY FOR ANOTHER

You can exchange one annuity for another without causing yourself tax problems. Section 1035 of the Internal Revenue Code allows for the tax free exchange of one annuity contract for another. It's a way out if you're unhappy with the rate of return on a fixed annuity or you're concerned about the financial health of the insurance company from which you purchased the annuity. Although you won't have a tax problem because of the exchange, you still have the surrender charge to consider.

HOME EQUITY

E*ven if you're emotionally attached to your home, you don't have to say good-bye to all of those memories just because you need cash. The equity in your home can, instead, be a source of ready cash in retirement.*

HOME EQUITY LOANS

A home equity loan offers some advantages.

Two ways. You have the choice of:

- Taking a lump sum through a second mortgage or by refinancing your first mortgage and taking out cash;
- Taking a home equity line of credit, borrow only when you need cash, and repay it like a credit card.

Tax break. The interest you pay may be tax deductible. Ask your tax advisor.

Low rates. Because the loan is secured by your home, the rate is typically lower than other types of loans.

Less risk. You can use the loan instead of cashing in stocks at the wrong time or withdrawing from an IRA. Both of those may result in tax consequences.

SELLING THE HOME

You can raise cash by selling your home, especially if it no longer meets your needs and you can downsize comfortably. For example, you may sell because you:

- Can't afford the upkeep or simply don't want the hassles;
- No longer have children living at home;
- Have lower income and the property tax deduction isn't worth as much to you;
- Are ready to move to another area or a different climate entirely.

23 Don't forget that when you borrow money against your equity, you're agreeing to a lien against your home.

REVERSE MORTGAGES

In contrast to a typical mortgage, the reverse mortgage pays you each month instead of you making a monthly payment. The lender is repaid from the proceeds when the home is sold. Reverse mortgages provide needed cash to retirees by lending them money at a lower cost than other loans.

The loan can be distributed to you in one (or a combination) of four ways:

- A lump sum;
- A line of credit that lets you take cash advances whenever necessary up to a limit;
- You receive monthly cash payments for as long as you live in the house;
- The loan proceeds are used to buy an annuity which will make payments for the rest of your life, even if you no longer live in the house.

Reverse mortgage programs differ from lender to lender. Therefore, the cash you can receive and the costs will differ. Shop around for the best program. Two programs to consider are:

- **Home Equity Conversion Mortgage.** Offered by the U.S. Department of Housing and Urban Development (HUD);
- **Fannie Mae Homekeeper Program.** Fannie Mae is an agency of the federal government.

Eligibility. Eligibility requirements may vary from lender to lender. These four are usually required to qualify for a reverse mortgage:

- You must be at least 62;
- You must own your own home;
- The home must be the principal residence you live in for more than half the year;
- All loans against the house must be paid off before getting the reverse mortgage or paid off with the first cash advance.

Amount. The amount you can borrow depends on a variety of factors, such as:

- **Age.** The older you are, the more money you may expect to receive since it's likely to be paid back more quickly;
- **Value.** The more your home is worth, the more you may be able to borrow;
- **Location.** The lender is more likely to be repaid on homes in desirable locations;
- **Interest rate.** When rates are low, you can often borrow more.

You will never owe more than the value of the home. The loan must be repaid when you die, sell the house, or move.

GROWING WHAT YOU HAVE

Most retirees shy away from investments that will grow their money. They believe they need to protect their money at this stage of life. Growing your money, however, may make a big difference in your retirement lifestyle

WHY GROW MONEY?

*I*n order to reach your goals, you may need to grow some of your assets, instead of putting them in conservative investments. Here's why.

WHY CONSERVATIVE INVESTING IS RISKY

Even with safe investments, you take a risk by investing too conservatively. Here are some reasons.

Inflation. Your investment may not keep pace with inflation. Even when the inflation rate is low, you might lose purchasing power, leaving your income insufficient to support your lifestyle.

Exhaustion. You may run out of money. According to one insurer's life expectancy table, 70% of men will die at ages ranging from 74 to 94. Among women, 70% will die between ages 77 and 96. If you plan for a short retirement and don't grow your nest egg, you may run out of money prematurely. Thanks to advances in medicine, you may see the day when your children retire and ask to borrow this book.

A DIFFERENT KIND OF INVESTMENT

Income investments usually involve lending money in return for interest. Growth investments involve ownership of an asset that may increase in value. Stock is the most popular growth investment. You assume the benefits and the risks of ownership in a company.

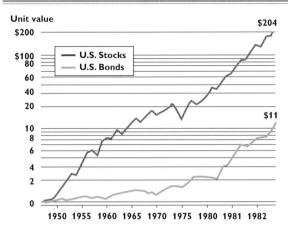

Unit value

Legend:
— U.S. Stocks
— U.S. Bonds

$204

$11

1950 1955 1960 1965 1970 1975 1980 1981 1982

◀ **STOCKS OUTPERFORM**

Even excluding the spectacular price increases of the 90's, stocks have historically outperformed bonds. This chart compares the growth of the S&P 500 index (stocks) to the growth of a combination of the Lehman Brothers Long Term High Quality Government/ Corporate Bond Index and S&P 500 High Grade Corporate Bond Index (bonds).

WHY SEEK GROWTH?

Many retirees shy away from attempting to grow money. Here's why it's an effective strategy, even in retirement:

● You still may have a long time horizon. For example, some of your money won't be needed for five years or longer;

● Growth investments have historically provided the best long-term opportunity to maintain and improve financial well-being;

● You will have more money available for loved ones and charity. Even if you have more than enough money to support your lifestyle, growth investments probably got you where you are now and give you a better opportunity to build your estate.

OPTIONS IF YOU CAN'T GET BY ON YOUR WITHDRAWALS

Many experts say that to keep your assets for 25 years or more, you should withdraw no more than 4% of the asset's initial value each year (plus an adjustment for inflation). But what if taking 4% a year doesn't meet your needs? Here are some options:

● Cut your living expenses;

● Returning to the work force on a full- or part-time basis;

● Increase your investment income. A different investment mix might permit you to withdraw a larger percentage.

24 Younger retirees, in particular, may need long-term growth investments.

TYPES OF GROWTH INVESTMENTS

When it comes to growth, stocks and mutual funds are the main types of vehicles investors use to achieve their goals. Be sure you understand the investments you're buying before sending any money.

STOCKS

Many companies are owned by people like you. To go public, a company divides its ownership into equal shares and sells them to the public. If you own its stock, you share in the success if it does well, and in the failure if it doesn't. In short, most people buy stock to let their fortunes ride with the fortunes of the company.

There are many types of stocks. These types aren't created to meet an investing need. Instead, they reflect the types of companies in the world and their various stages of development. Here are some of the different types of stocks:

Speculative stocks. These are start-up, or relatively new companies who have not yet established themselves in their product or service market. They may also be companies in high risk businesses, such as the Internet, biotechnology, and a number of other highly competitive and money-intensive industries.

Growth stocks. These are companies that have moved beyond the phase of uncertainty and have proven growth patterns, but still have a lot of room to grow. The more and faster they grow, the more stock price movement investors can expect to see.

Value stocks. These are well-established companies with histories of consistent earnings and growth. Many value stocks are also referred to as blue-chip stocks.

STOCK MUTUAL FUNDS

Mutual funds have a variety of investment objectives. Here are some of the possibilities if growth is your objective.

Aggressive growth funds. The fund manager doesn't hesitate to buy stocks that are volatile or those with high P/E (price-to-earnings) ratios. This ratio compares the price of the stock to the company's current earnings. S/he is looking for stocks that have a chance to build a significant amount of earnings in the future. The fund manager is looking for capital appreciation in a very short period of time.

Growth funds. These funds invest in stocks with good prospects for future earnings growth. Although their futures looks strong to the fund manager, the stocks invested in usually have high price-to-earnings ratios and low dividend payouts. A growth fund manager may restrict investments to small, mid-size, or large companies.

Growth-and-income funds. The fund manager focuses on two areas when selecting stocks, the potential for price appreciation and current income. These funds typically try to create a balance between growth and income. They are often referred to as *balanced funds*.

Value funds. The fund manager invests in stocks that are undervalued. The stocks will have low price-to-earnings (P/E) ratios. Stocks with lower P/E ratios are the most appealing to the fund manager. A value fund manager may limit investments to small, mid-size, or large companies.

Index funds. Index funds attempt to mimic the performance of a market index, such as the S&P 500 or the Russell 2000. To achieve this, the fund holds all or a sample of the stocks that comprise a particular index. Index funds are generally tax-friendly because they hold trading to a minimum.

Foreign stock funds. These funds are for investors who don't want to rely completely on the health of the American economy. The fund manager invests in foreign stocks, mostly from companies in Asia and Europe.

Emerging market funds. These may be even more volatile, because the companies they invest in are in countries that are less stable. These funds are generally considered riskier than foreign funds that invest in more developed countries.

25 Time lowers stock risk. Over any ten-year period, stocks have outperformed all other types of investments.

MANAGING YOUR MONEY

You now have some idea of what types of investments are attractive to you. Next you need to select strategies you are comfortable with. This chapter will help you understand what's involved in selecting the right strategy for you.

THE ROLE OF TIME

J ust because you're retired doesn't mean you don't have time to invest for the future. With a little luck, you will have a long life ahead of you and your investments still have time to grow.

LIQUIDITY

When managing your money in retirement, you need to be liquid, so you're not forced to sell off assets during a bear market. *Liquidity* refers to the ability to convert investments into cash without losing your principal.

How do you decide how much to allocate to quick cash, income producing investments that will sustain at least a portion of your needs for the remaining years? A good rule of thumb is that you should keep three to five years of living expenses in fixed income investments and ready cash. The remainder can be put in stocks and other investments that have the potential for appreciation.

TIMETABLE FOR STOCK INVESTMENTS

The volatility of the stock market is most dangerous if you anticipate needing your money back soon. You risk cashing in at a bad time. Here's what many experts recommend:

● If you need the money within a year, consider "parking" the amount you anticipate needing in a money market fund, not the stock market;

● If you have five years, consider putting some money in stocks;

● If you have a ten-year window, consider increasing the percentage you have in stocks;

● If you have over ten years, most of your money may be appropriate for stock investing.

Everyone's situation is different, so seek advice if necessary.

COMPOUNDING

With time on your side, you can still take advantage of the power of compounding. Compounding enables you to earn money on your original investment and on the earnings from that investment. Time enhances the power of compounding. Your time horizon is the time between now and when you anticipate needing the money.

MORE TO SUPPORT YOU ▶
The less you withdraw from your savings, the more you will have growing for you.

VOLATILITY

Depending upon your perspective, volatility can be good or bad. The volatility of an investment is its potential for large gains or losses. Some stocks go up significantly during boom years and down enormously during bad times. Some stocks go down and never recover. You can never really predict.

The more years you have until you will need the money, the less you need to be concerned with the ups and downs of your investments' prices. In fact, stocks, which as a group are typically the most volatile investments, have outperformed every other type of investment in any ten-year period since the 1920s.

SHIFTING ASSETS

S ome people believe that the best way to protect money is by giving it away. Shifting assets helps you protect funds you might lose anyway.

REASONS FOR SHIFTING ASSETS

Shifting assets means moving them from one place to another. For example, you might move money from a regular investment account to a trust account. Thanks to the soaring stock market and rising real estate prices, many middle-income taxpayers have estates that may be subject to taxes. There are also inheritance taxes to consider in some states, as well as income taxes on retirement accounts. Asset shifting has been used for many purposes:

- Hiding assets from a spouse in a divorce action;
- Estate planning;
- Keeping assets from creditors and plaintiffs;
- Tax reduction;
- To qualify for benefits and aid from the government and other sources.

SHIFTING ASSETS AS PART OF ESTATE PLANNING

Asset shifting is particularly effective as a way to reduce the size of your estate and avoid taxes. In the year 2000, a taxpayer has an exemption of $675,000 from federal estate taxes. That may seem like a lot of money, but it's not if you consider that these assets are considered to be part of your taxable estate:

- House;
- All personal property;
- Cars and boats;
- Life insurance proceeds;
- IRAs, 401(k)s, and other types of retirement accounts;
- Bank accounts, stocks, and bonds.

▼ **WHERE IS IT ALL STORED?**
All of your assets are in accounts of one kind or another. Think of those accounts as storage places for your items of value, each with a tag that identifies who has the rights to those particular assets. As your life changes with the seasons, you may decide there are advantages to changing your storage places.

26 You can shift assets quite effectively with a trust. Even though you shift an asset with a trust, you can retain the income for yourself or a dependent.

GIFTS

You can give away as much as $10,000 each year to anyone without paying taxes. They don't have to be related to you. Your spouse can also give up to $10,000 per year to any or all of the same people. The gifts are nontaxable.

Gifts can help you reduce your taxable estate to a level that is free of federal estate taxes. However, giving away this money may leave the person short of funds if s/he develops an incapacitating illness. An individual may require years of expensive care. One option is to buy long-term care insurance and then begin making gifts.

Now is a good time to be thinking of charitable gifts as well. They can help your tax situation now and when you die, not to mention the good deed you would be doing.

BENEFITS OF ESTATE PLANNING

Estate planning can help avoid or minimize these problems:
- A huge income tax bill when you inherit an IRA;
- Probate—the legal process of distributing your property.;
- Federal estate taxes;
- State inheritance taxes.

LEAVING ASSETS TO YOUR SPOUSE

Suppose a married couple has about $1,000,000 in assets. If one spouse dies there's an unlimited marital deduction which allows the transfer of any amount directly to the surviving spouse free of estate taxes. The problem arises, however, when the surviving spouse wants to distribute that $1,000,000 estate to the couple's children. The estate is now worth more than the $675,000 exemption from federal estate taxes. Consult a trust and estate attorney.

27 Some asset shifting is perfectly legal, while other maneuvers are illegal and unethical. Be sure you understand the differences.

ASSET ALLOCATION

F inancial experts recommend an investment strategy called asset allocation. To pursue this strategy, you divide your investments among different types of assets such as stocks, bonds, and cash. There are several reasons why this strategy is recommended by so many.

WHAT IT IS

Your goal is to create a mix of investments that will be profitable over the long-term. By using asset allocation, investors can meet or exceed their investment goals with less risk.

Essentially, you're diversifying your investment portfolio, which is a way of reducing risk. But it's not just a case of having a percentage of each different asset class. For example, the percentage of your portfolio in the stock market could be divided among different funds with different goals. There are several assets that belong in your portfolio:

- Stocks and stock mutual funds;
- Bonds and bond mutual funds;
- Cash and money market funds;
- Real estate.

Reduced risks. Asset allocation reduces the risk that you have too much money tied up in one particular investment, such as a stock. Since your portfolio is spread out among various asset classes, the odds are usually less that all of them will be performing badly.

RULE OF THUMB

The old method. There used to be a rule-of-thumb that financial planners employed to determine the right mix of investments for a client. You subtract the individual's age from 100 to determine the percentage of assets that should be allocated in the stock market. With this rule-of-thumb, if you're 60 years old, 40% of your funds should be in stock, since 100 less 60 equals 40. A 40 year old should have 60% of his funds in stock, since 100 less 40 equals 60.

New ideas. That rule-of-thumb has lost favor, because individuals age 60 or older can't necessarily be too conservative in their investing. They may have 30 or more years ahead of them and need to invest to keep up with inflation. Nevertheless, older investors need to be liquid, so they don't have to liquidate their stock portfolio during a bear market. Another problem with rules-of-thumb such as these is that not all stock investments are risky. Investing in blue-chip stocks is usually considered a lot less risky than buying speculative stocks.

WHY ALLOCATE?

Proponents of the asset allocation strategy believe that investment success isn't necessarily the result of which investment you choose, but possibly even more on what percentages you've allocated among the different asset classes—stocks, bonds, and cash. Other types include real estate and hard assets like gold.

The right mix of investments for you depends upon these factors:

- Your age;
- Your financial circumstances;
- Your risk tolerance;
- Your goals.

REBALANCING: WHAT IT IS

Once you have the right mix of investments, you need to make sure they stay in balance. For instance, a stock fund may grow significantly and then represent too large a percentage of your portfolio. Rebalancing means selling some of the asset class that grows too large and buying more of the asset classes that are proportionately smaller.

WHY REBALANCE?

There are several reasons for rebalancing:

- If your stock funds grow significantly, they may represent too large a percentage of your portfolio, increasing your risk because your portfolio is now less diversified;
- Your needs change. For example, the typical retiree needs a steady stream of income and may move some of his or her money to bonds and stocks that pay dividends. As you get closer to retirement age, your investment horizon shrinks and it may be time to rebalance your portfolio with an emphasis on liquidity.

ASSET ALLOCATION FUNDS

These funds can solve your asset allocation dilemma. They invest to achieve a mix of investments that's right for someone with your investment objectives and risk temperament. The investment manager rebalances the portfolio if there are significant changes in the market values of the assets to maintain as steady a mix as possible.

WHO CAN HELP?

No matter how independent you are or care to be, don't
be embarrassed to ask for help. Sometimes, this assistance
will cost you money, but it's usually a good investment.
Make sure, however, that the people helping you
have your best interests at heart.

FINANCIAL PLANNERS

Just like almost anyone can call him or herself a consultant, almost anyone can say s/he's a financial planner. When you're in the market for a planner, try to separate the true professionals from those who merely dabble in the field.

28 Many insurance agents and brokers call themselves financial planners, but they aren't the right person to turn to for objective financial planning advice.

FINDING THE RIGHT ONE

There are ways to find a good financial advisor:

- Get referrals from family, friends, and business associates;
- Look at the person's educational credentials. The Certified Financial Planner (CFP) designation means the person has completed numerous courses in the field and subscribes to a strict code of ethics. Some CPAs have additional training and are known as Personal Financial Specialists;
- Look for someone who's an established member of the community;
- Meet with the planner and ask questions.

QUESTIONS TO ASK A POTENTIAL FINANCIAL ADVISOR

Whatever their fee structure, it's important that you're told up-front how the planner is compensated. Aside from asking about fees, here are some other important questions to ask:

- Are you registered with the Securities and Exchange Commission?
- What is your investment philosophy?
- What are your educational credentials?
- Is this your full-time job?
- How do you keep up-to-date on financial planning issues?
- What is your experience with tax issues, relating to retirement?

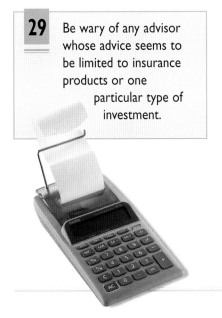

29 Be wary of any advisor whose advice seems to be limited to insurance products or one particular type of investment.

HOW FINANCIAL PLANNERS ARE COMPENSATED

Financial planners make money in one of three ways or in a combination of the three.

Fee-only. Fee-only planners earn no commission from the products they recommend and so may be less biased. Their fee is established in advance. You might pay by the hour or the session.

Percentage of your assets. Some planners manage your portfolio and take a percentage of the assets they manage for you.

Commission. Some planners earn commissions on products they recommend. Although it may seem like you're getting free counseling, you won't necessarily be getting objective advice. The planner may be inclined to recommend products that pay the best commission.

CONTACTS

Some organizations to contact for recommendations of planners in your area include:

- Certified Financial Planner Board of Standards (888-237-6275; www.cfpboard.org);
- The American Institute of CPAs, PFS Division (888-777-7077; www.cpapfs.org);
- Financial Planning Association (800-282-7526; www.fpanet.org).

INSURANCE AGENTS

*I*nsurance needs change at various stages of our life. In retirement, you still need to be absolutely sure you have the right coverage for your particular situation. One thing never changes: You need to have an insurance agent who is looking out for your needs, not his or her need to make a commission. Your insurance portfolio can be every bit as important as your investment portfolio. Take a look at your insurance coverage in all of these key areas.

AUTO INSURANCE

Unless you're ready to turn over the keys and the title, you need to make sure you have adequate coverage on your car. Damage awards have grown over the years, so those $100,000 liability limits are inadequate. It's very inexpensive to raise those limits by several hundred thousand dollars. Make sure your property damage limits are sufficient too. Ask your agent about what discounts are available. You should pay less because you're driving less and not commuting to work each day. If you're driving an old car that isn't worth much, consider dropping the collision coverage. You should get a discount for driving a car with air bags, anti-lock brakes, and built-in anti-theft systems.

HOW TO EVALUATE YOUR AGENT

Any *good* insurance agent will have these characteristics:

- They know it's in their long-term interest to find you the right coverage at the right price;
- They won't sell you any unnecessary coverage;
- They admit when you're better off using a different agent to sell you a policy;
  - They're every bit as helpful and responsive when you have a claim as they are when you're buying a policy.

HOMEOWNER'S INSURANCE

Whether you live in a house or condo, make sure you have adequate homeowner's coverage. As with auto insurance, you will need enough liability coverage to protect your assets if someone gets hurt on your property or because of your negligence.

LIFE INSURANCE

Generally, your need for life insurance declines as you get older, since your children no longer depend upon you for support. Nevertheless, life insurance is an important estate planning tool.

HEALTH INSURANCE

Medicare isn't enough coverage to have. Unless you receive supplemental coverage through your former employer's health plan, consider buying a Medicare supplemental policy. It picks up many expenses that Medicare won't pay. There's also a relatively new program called Medicare + Choice that combines Medicare and supplemental coverage. The HMO you enroll with provides all of your Medicare-covered services, along with other care that might typically be covered by a Medicare supplement.

LONG-TERM CARE INSURANCE

As mentioned earlier, Medicare, Medicare supplemental policies, and Medicare + Choice do not cover long-term care, except in very limited circumstances. Long-term care insurance is a specialized field and your current carrier may not offer this coverage.

WARNING: CHURNING

Churning is when an agent tries to convince you to turn in one perfectly good policy for another. The agent gets a new commission when the policy is replaced and you may lose valuable benefits accrued under the existing policy. Replacement is always good for the agent, but not necessarily good for you. Many large life insurance companies were sanctioned recently by insurance regulators for churning by their agents.

BUYER BEWARE

Beware of insurance policies that only protect against one disease. Typically, these policies only pay while you're hospitalized.

PERSONAL LIABILITY

A huge lawsuit can take away many of the assets you're living on in retirement. For a few hundred dollars, you can increase your protection against lawsuits of $1,000,000 or more. An *umbrella policy* also increases the coverage you have under your auto and homeowner's policies and covers other potential lawsuits such as a slander action against you.

TRUST AND ESTATE ATTORNEYS

*O*ffice supply stores are filled with do-it-yourself wills and other legal documents. You can buy software to prepare simple wills and trusts. There are even books that try to explain every legal aspect of estate planning. But some matters should be left in the hands of the professionals.

HOW TO FIND THE RIGHT ONE

Whether you're a do-it-yourself type or not, everyone needs a will at a minimum. Unless you have the simplest of estates, you probably need to seek the services of a legal professional. Furthermore, you might even need someone who specializes in estates and trusts, because some attorneys aren't familiar with all of the nuances of estate planning. Much like the choice of any professional, here are some suggestions for finding the right person:

- You should seek recommendations from people you trust;
- You should look for someone who has extensive experience with estate planning issues and who specializes in these matters. The attorney who handles your business affairs isn't necessarily the right person to help you with estate planning;
- Some government offices keep records of complaints against attorneys. Check with these offices if you have doubts about an attorney.

WHAT THEY DO

Trust and estate attorneys help you make sure that your property winds up in the hands of the people you choose to receive it. They prepare legal documents that will carry out your wishes now and after you die. These lawyers also try to minimize the taxes owed when your property is distributed.

 30 The phone book or a television commercial isn't the way to choose an attorney.

IT'S A FACT

According to AARP, only 60% of Americans age 50 and older have a will.

WHY PEOPLE PUT OFF ESTATE PLANNING

People put off estate planning for several reasons:

● You think your assets are modest;
● You've never really added up how much your estate is worth;
● You assume you have plenty of time to begin the estate planning process;
● You misunderstand which property is part of your estate. For example, life insurance proceeds go directly to beneficiaries without going through probate, the legal process for settling your estate. Even though beneficiaries won't pay income taxes on life insurance proceeds, they're considered to be part of the estate. A $500,000 death benefit won't leave much room for other assets if the exemption from federal estate taxes is limited to $675,000;
● You're afraid the money might be needed to pay the high cost of long-term care.

QUESTIONS TO ASK A POTENTIAL LAWYER

There are some important questions to ask in order to select the right estate planning attorney:

● Do you specialize in the estate planning area?
● What percentage of your practice is devoted to estate planning issues?
● What degrees and advanced degrees do you hold?
● Will you work in conjunction with my financial planner and accountant?
● Do you charge a flat fee or do you bill hourly?
● How much do you estimate that my estate planning will cost?
● What information can I provide that will hold down the cost?

You would be wise to interview several estate planning attorneys before deciding on one.

BROKERAGE FIRMS

T hanks to the Internet, many people are becoming extremely knowledgeable about companies and investments. Some are researching investment opportunities themselves and even trading stocks on the Internet. However, a lot of people still rely on others for help in making their investment decisions.

TYPES OF BROKERS

According to the Forum for Investor Advice in Bethesda, Maryland, roughly 2/3 of retirees with a computer use it to check out the performance of their investments.

Of that group, only 11 percent have ever used the Internet to trade stocks or bonds. They turn instead to stockbrokers for assistance. There are two types of brokers:

● Full-service brokers;
● Discount brokers.

A stockbroker is licensed by the Securities and Exchange Commission (SEC), as well as state securities regulators, to sell investments. They earn most of their living from commissions. Full-service brokers give advice, recommend strategies, and provide research recommendations. If you don't need advice and do the research yourself, you might want to use a discount broker. Discount brokers earn less of a commission and usually don't recommend specific securities.

SUITABILITY REQUIREMENTS

An ethical broker will always be concerned with suitability issues. The broker should never recommend any investment that isn't suitable for someone with your investment temperament. Suitability requires that the registered representative make certain the investment meets two requirements:

● It must be appropriate;
● It must be consistent with the client's objectives.

You can invest in any investment you choose, but the broker must warn you when it's unsuitable for you.

IT'S A FACT

In 1999, 36% of all mutual fund assets were held in retirement plans.

ADDITIONAL PROGRAMS AND INFORMATION

You can draw on the Internet for information on money management. Here are some website suggestions:

- American Savings Education Council: www.asec.org and www.choosetosave.org;
- Employee Benefit Research Institute: www.ebri.org;
- Federal Trade Commission: www.consumer.gov;
- Housing and Urban Development (HUD): www.hud.gov/rvrsmort.html; 202-708-2700;
- National Center for Home Equity Conversion: www.reverse.org;
- Securities and Exchange Commission: www.sec.gov;
- Small Business Administration: www.sbaonline.gov;
- Social Security Administration: www.ssa.gov/retire; 800-772-1213.

HOW TO INVESTIGATE A BROKER

It always pays to fully investigate a broker before depending upon the person for advice. Before dealing with a broker, take these steps to check out his or her credibility and track record:

- Ask for the broker's Central Registration Depository (CRD) number;
- Call your state's securities regulators;
- Contact the National Association of Securities Dealers. Its website is www.nasd.com or call 800-289-9999;
- Ask the broker for the names of clients you might contact.

A WEALTH OF EDUCATION

As an SEC official recently said, "An investor can enter a website, check the market, read about investing for retirement, order a paper copy of a prospectus, use a calculator to evaluate asset allocation, review recent press releases, purchase shares in one portfolio and redeem shares in another—all before breakfast." Even if you prefer books and newspapers to the Internet, educating yourself is key to managing your money in retirement.

SCAMS AND FRAUDS

The SEC estimates that investors are losing as much as $10 billion a year to securities fraud. Often, fraudulent schemes are successful because investors are obsessed with making a quick buck.

RED FLAGS

Retirees find themselves on the mailing and call list of companies selling almost every type of product and service. Some salespeople will even come to your door. These red flags should make you suspicious of the company making the sales pitch. Here are some red flags:

- High-pressure sales pitches;
- Nothing is in writing;
- No return phone number;
- A decision must be made immediately;
- Demands for cash or a credit card number.

31 Contact the FTC at 877-382-4357 for a complaint form if you suspect telemarketing fraud (www.consumer.gov/knowfraud).

32 Don't let a salesperson enter your home unless you've arranged the meeting in advance and the person has proper identification.

▼ **DON'T BE FOOLED**
Sweepstakes, telemarketing, and snake oil salesman target retirees. Check out anything that sounds too good to be true. You could save yourself a lot of grief and money. According to AARP, the U.S. Department of Justice estimates that one out of six consumers is cheated each year by fraudulent telemarketers. Many of those calls are aimed at older consumers.

SWEEPSTAKES
YOU HAVE WON
$1,000,000

SOME SCAM AREAS

Here are some of the most common scams:

- Pre-need funeral contracts;
- Cemetery plots;
- Long-term care insurance, Medigap policies, and medical plans;
- Investments.

SCAMS TO WATCH OUT FOR

Along with the scams that have been around for years, there are new ones each day. Don't let your guard down, especially when you find yourself in these situations:

- Watch out for calls from boiler rooms filled with aggressive salespeople selling bogus investments;
- The phone rings during dinner saying you won a contest or you get a postcard telling you how to claim your prize. If you win a contest, you will be notified by an official letter, not a phone call or a post card sent bulk mail. Understand whether a vacation you've won is a come-on for a time share;
- Advance fee loan companies guarantee a low interest rate loan if you pay a fee. After you pay it, the company rarely comes through with the loan;
- Fast-talking salespeople will try to sell you just about anything. Avoid getting talked into home improvements, roof repairs, and other services you don't need.

HOW TO AVOID BECOMING A VICTIM

As you get older, the danger of becoming a victim increases. Whether it's a store clerk who purposely gives you the wrong change or fraud on the Internet, there are steps you can take to avoid being cheated:

- Deal only with people you know and trust;
- Don't let people rush you into making decisions;
- Don't leave the counter or sign on the dotted line until you're satisfied with the explanation given;
- Ask your children or a trusted friend for assistance with major decisions;
- Avoid giving your Social Security number to anyone. More than 500,000 Social Security numbers are stolen each year;
- Thoroughly review your credit card and bank statements each month, looking for suspicious activity;
- Use some of your free time to stay organized and keep meticulous records;
- Check with government agencies before dealing with a company or individual;
- Buy a shredder to get rid of documents with personal information;
- If you go on the Internet, monitor your "cookies," which create a profile of the websites you're visiting. To learn more about them, and delete them if you decide that's best for you, check out www.cookiecentral.com.

WHERE TO GO FOR HELP

There are public and private groups that offer advice to senior citizens, as well as assistance if a problem occurs.

CONSUMER PROTECTION AGENCIES

These agencies might be part of your state or county government. Usually, investigators from this office will look into consumer complaints against businesses.

Insurance department. Every state has an insurance department, or a similar agency, that regulates the sale of insurance. Normally, you can file complaints against insurance agents and companies that are not treating you fairly. You can also get advice before you buy a policy. Sometimes, the insurance department also monitors HMOs. Many insurance departments keep a record of complaints against agents and insurers.

Department of Health. Problems with HMOs are often resolved by the Department of Health. They may also be responsible for monitoring nursing homes, physicians, and hospitals. The Department might also address quality of care and other healthcare issues. Some state health departments can provide valuable information on the quality of nursing homes and assisted living residences.

Comptroller's Office. This department of state government is likely to address banking and finance company issues.

33 AARP is a leading activist voice for seniors. Call (800) 424-3410, or visit www.aarp.org.

YOU'VE GOT ▶ THE POWER!
Just because you're getting older, doesn't mean you're becoming defenseless.

TAKING MATTERS INTO YOUR OWN HANDS

Sometimes, you will have to take matters into your own hands. Here are some avenues to take if you've been wronged and the government watchdogs aren't able to help. There are normally ways to redress your legal rights without a lawyer.

Small claims court. Unlike most legal proceedings, the laws of evidence and the procedural rules are not very strict. The jurisdiction of a small claims court will depend upon where you live. Usually, you won't be able to bring an action if the damages are above a particular amount.

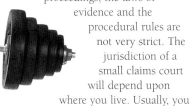

Better Business Bureau (BBB). The Better Business Bureau in your area may have an arbitration program available to resolve disputes between consumers and participating businesses. At a minimum, check with the BBB before getting work done on your home or becoming involved in a business transaction.

Newspaper and television consumer reporters. In every city, there's usually a columnist in the newspaper or a television personality who attempts to resolve consumer problems. These individuals are often able to achieve results, because of the potential for negative publicity.

STATE AGENCIES

There are organizations in every state that can assist retirees and other consumers with problems. The nature of your problem determines which office has jurisdiction.

Attorney general. The state attorney general will usually have jurisdiction over complaints alleging fraud or misrepresentation. The attorney general may help to resolve complaints against car dealers and administer a Lemon Law Program.

Securities Commission. This state office might also be available to help you check on brokers and investment advisors.

GOVERNMENT AGENCIES

There are many agencies that can assist you with a problem.

Federal Trade Commission. The Federal Trade Commission can help consumers with issues ranging from product recalls to identity theft. See www.consumer.gov.

Securities and Exchange Commission (SEC). If your stockbroker makes an error, you can complain to the SEC. Before going to the SEC, however, try to resolve any issues with the firm's branch manager and work your way through the management hierarchy. A dispute can also be resolved through arbitration.

ASSISTANCE PROGRAMS

I f a modest Social Security check is your only source of income in retirement, living from day to day will be a struggle. According to EBRI, 25% of retirees on Social Security have total income that is below the poverty level. There are other benefits available to retirees who are in dire financial straits.

SUPPLEMENTAL SECURITY INCOME BENEFITS (SSI)

SSI benefits are not based upon past earnings and are financed by general tax revenues. The purpose of these benefits is to assure a minimum monthly income for elderly and disabled individuals.

With SSI, the federal government pays the basic rate. Some states add money to the federal government's payment. You can check with your local Social Security office to determine your eligibility and the SSI benefit available in your state.

IT'S A FACT

A booming economy and a slow-down of spending has extended the life of the Medicare trust fund to 2023.

MEDICAID

Medicaid is a federal program, administered by the states, that pays for care of individuals with low income or those who meet certain guidelines. Medicaid often pays for care that isn't covered by Medicare, such as custodial care in a nursing home.

You're not likely to qualify for Medicaid if you have significant savings or assets. Often, you're not eligible until you've exhausted those assets. There are laws making it extremely difficult to transfer assets to a spouse in order to qualify for Medicaid. Nevertheless, protection is built into the Medicaid laws, so your spouse won't become impoverished.

FOOD STAMPS

This type of assistance helps pay the food bill of retirees meeting certain income restrictions. The Child and Adult Care Food Program is an underutilized federal entitlement program for communities striving to offer safe and supportive after-school programs for children while their parents work. For useful articles and resources visit www.povertylaw.org/articles/headings/food.htm

OTHER ASSISTANCE

In almost every area, there are special programs available for retirees. Some require low income for eligibility, while others don't. Most of these programs are government-sponsored. Others are financed by religious and community groups.

If you're struggling financially, don't hesitate to see what programs are available for someone in your situation. Check whether these services, or similar ones, are offered in your community:

● Meals-on-wheels for shut-ins;
● Adult day care;
● Energy assistance;
● Free or low-cost transportation to appointments with doctors;
● Assistance with tax return preparation;
● Property tax rebates;
● Subsidized housing.

FREE ACCESS

If you don't have access to the Internet, here are some useful phone numbers.

● National Center on Poverty Law, in Chicago at (312) 263-3830;
● Small Business Administration (SBA) federal assistance programs, at www.clarksburg.com/federal.htm;
● The Catalog of Domestic Assistance lists public aid programs at www.cfda.gov.

IT'S A FACT

In January 2001, the average Social Security check went from $804 to $831, an increase of 3.4% in benefits.

34 Internet access is free at your local public library.

INDEX

ACKNOWLEDGMENTS

AUTHORS' ACKNOWLEDGMENTS

The production of this book has called on the skills of many people. A special thanks to the sponsors and staff of the Employee Benefit Research Institute over the past 22 years, without whom this work would not be possible. We would also like to mention our editors at Dorling Kindersley, and our consultant, Nick Clemente. Marc wishes to dedicate this book to Zachary Robinson for his great patience and support when it was most needed. Special thanks to the Lloyd Family for lending their stunning family portrait, and to Teresa Clavasquin for her generous support and assistance.

PUBLISHER'S ACKNOWLEDGMENTS

Dorling Kindersley would like to thank everyone who worked on the Essential Finance series, and the following for their help and participation:

Editorial Stephanie Rubenstein; **Design and Layout** Jill Dupont; **Consultants** Nick Clemente; Skeeter; **Indexer** Rachel Rice; **Proofreader** Stephanie Rubenstein; **Photography** Anthony Nex; **Photographers' Assistants** Damon Dulas;**Models** Harold Rose, Eleanor Rose,Liza Steixner, Mimi Lieberman; **Picture Researcher** Mark Dennis; Sam Ruston

AUTHORS' BIOGRAPHIES

Dallas Salisbury is President and CEO of the Employee Benefit Research Institute (EBRI), in Washington, DC. EBRI was founded in 1978 to provide objective, unbiased information regarding the employee benefit system and related economic security issues. Dallas joined EBRI at its founding in 1978. Dallas is also chairman and CEO of the American Savings Education Council (ASEC), and the Consumer Health Education Council (CHEC). Both are partnerships of public and private-sector institutions that undertake initiatives to raise public awareness regarding what is needed to ensure long-term economic and health security. Dallas is a Fellow of the National Academy of Human Resources, the recipient of the 1997 Award for Professional Excellence from the Society for Human Resources Management and the 1998 Keystone Award of "WorldatWork." He has served on the Secretary of Labor's ERISA Advisory Council and the Presidential PBGC Advisory Committee. He currently serves as a member of the Advisory Committee to the Comptroller to the United States, the 2001 Board of Directors for the Society of Human Resource Management, and on the GAO Advisory Group on Social Security and Retirement. Prior to joining EBRI, Dallas held full-time positions with the Washington State Legislature, the U.S. Department of Justice, the Pension Benefit Guaranty Corporation (PBGC), and the Pension and Welfare Benefits Administration of the U.S. Department of Labor. He holds a B.A. degree in finance from the University of Washington and an M.A. in public policy and administration from the Maxwell School at Syracuse University.

Marc Robinson is co-founder of Internet-based moneytours.com, a personal finance resource for corporations, universities, credit unions, and other institutions interested in helping their constituents make intelligent decisions about their financial lives. He wrote the original *The Wall Street Journal Guide to Understanding Money and Markets*, created *The Wall Street Journal Guide to Understanding Personal Finance*, co-published a personal finance series with Time Life Books, and wrote a children's book about onomateopia in different languages. In his two decades in the financial services industry, Marc has provided marketing consulting to many top Wall Street firms. He is admitted to practice law in New York State.